On Time, Every Time

A Journal for Organized Bill Payment

Activinotes

Activinotes

DAILY JOURNALS, PLANNERS, NOTEBOOKS AND OTHER BLANK BOOKS

Name: _____

Address: _____

E-mail : _____

Contact no's : _____

_____

Bills Payment Schedule & List

PAID Yes/No	BILLS	DUE DATES	BUDGET	REALIZATION

NOTES

Bills Payment Schedule & List

PAID Yes/No	BILLS	DUE DATES	BUDGET	REALIZATION

NOTES

{MONTHLY BUDGET}

STARTING BALANCE	STARTING DEBT	MONTHLY INCOME

{EXPENSES}

HOUSING	BUDGET	SPENT	TRANSPORTATION	BUDGET	SPENT
Rent/Mortgage			Car Payment		
Taxes			Car Insurance		
Insurance			Gas		
Repairs			Maintenance		
Total			Total		

UTILITIES	BUDGET	SPENT	PERSONAL	BUDGET	SPENT
Electricity			Entertainment		
Gas			Clothing		
Sewer/Trash			Kids Stuff		
Internet			Cosmetic		
Phone			Medical		
Total			Total		

FOOD	BUDGET	SPENT	MEDICAL	BUDGET	SPENT
Grocery			Doctor Bills		
Restaurants			Medication		
Total			Total		

CHARITY	BUDGET	SPENT	DEBTS	BUDGET	SPENT
Tithes			CC 1		
Charity			CC 2		
Total			Total		

STARTING BALANCE	STARTING DEBT	MONTHLY INCOME

{FILE IT}

MONEY

TAXES

MEDICAL

HOME

AUTO

BUSINESS

Bills Payment Schedule & List

PAID Yes/No	BILLS	DUE DATES	BUDGET	REALIZATION

NOTES

Bills Payment Schedule & List

PAID Yes/No	BILLS	DUE DATES	BUDGET	REALIZATION

NOTES

{MONTHLY BUDGET}

STARTING BALANCE	STARTING DEBT	MONTHLY INCOME
_____	_____	_____

{EXPENSES}

HOUSING	BUDGET	SPENT	TRANSPORTATION	BUDGET	SPENT
Rent/Mortgage			Car Payment		
Taxes			Car Insurance		
Insurance			Gas		
Repairs			Maintenance		
Total			Total		

UTILITIES	BUDGET	SPENT	PERSONAL	BUDGET	SPENT
Electricity			Entertainment		
Gas			Clothing		
Sewer/Trash			Kids Stuff		
Internet			Cosmetic		
Phone			Medical		
Total			Total		

FOOD	BUDGET	SPENT	MEDICAL	BUDGET	SPENT
Grocery			Doctor Bills		
Restaurants			Medication		
Total			Total		

CHARITY	BUDGET	SPENT	DEBTS	BUDGET	SPENT
Tithes			CC 1		
Charity			CC 2		
Total			Total		

STARTING BALANCE	STARTING DEBT	MONTHLY INCOME
_____	_____	_____

{FILE IT}

MONEY

TAXES

MEDICAL

HOME

AUTO

BUSINESS

Bills Payment Schedule & List

PAID Yes/No	BILLS	DUE DATES	BUDGET	REALIZATION

NOTES

_____

_____

_____

_____

_____

_____

Bills Payment Schedule & List

PAID Yes/No	BILLS	DUE DATES	BUDGET	REALIZATION

NOTES

{MONTHLY BUDGET}

STARTING BALANCE	STARTING DEBT	MONTHLY INCOME

{EXPENSES}

HOUSING	BUDGET	SPENT	TRANSPORTATION	BUDGET	SPENT
Rent/Mortgage			Car Payment		
Taxes			Car Insurance		
Insurance			Gas		
Repairs			Maintenance		
Total			Total		

UTILITIES	BUDGET	SPENT	PERSONAL	BUDGET	SPENT
Electricity			Entertainment		
Gas			Clothing		
Sewer/Trash			Kids Stuff		
Internet			Cosmetic		
Phone			Medical		
Total			Total		

FOOD	BUDGET	SPENT	MEDICAL	BUDGET	SPENT
Grocery			Doctor Bills		
Restaurants			Medication		
Total			Total		

CHARITY	BUDGET	SPENT	DEBTS	BUDGET	SPENT
Tithes			CC 1		
Charity			CC 2		
Total			Total		

STARTING BALANCE	STARTING DEBT	MONTHLY INCOME

{FILE IT}

MONEY

TAXES

MEDICAL

HOME

AUTO

BUSINESS

Bills Payment Schedule & List

PAID Yes/No	BILLS	DUE DATES	BUDGET	REALIZATION

NOTES

_____

_____

_____

_____

_____

_____

Bills Payment Schedule & List

PAID Yes/No	BILLS	DUE DATES	BUDGET	REALIZATION

NOTES

{MONTHLY BUDGET}

STARTING BALANCE	STARTING DEBT	MONTHLY INCOME

{EXPENSES}

HOUSING	BUDGET	SPENT	TRANSPORTATION	BUDGET	SPENT
Rent/Mortgage			Car Payment		
Taxes			Car Insurance		
Insurance			Gas		
Repairs			Maintenance		
Total			Total		

UTILITIES	BUDGET	SPENT	PERSONAL	BUDGET	SPENT
Electricity			Entertainment		
Gas			Clothing		
Sewer/Trash			Kids Stuff		
Internet			Cosmetic		
Phone			Medical		
Total			Total		

FOOD	BUDGET	SPENT	MEDICAL	BUDGET	SPENT
Grocery			Doctor Bills		
Restaurants			Medication		
Total			Total		

CHARITY	BUDGET	SPENT	DEBTS	BUDGET	SPENT
Tithes			CC 1		
Charity			CC 2		
Total			Total		

STARTING BALANCE	STARTING DEBT	MONTHLY INCOME

{FILE IT}

MONEY

TAXES

MEDICAL

HOME

AUTO

BUSINESS

Bills Payment Schedule & List

PAID Yes/No	BILLS	DUE DATES	BUDGET	REALIZATION

NOTES

_____

_____

_____

_____

_____

_____

Bills Payment Schedule & List

PAID Yes/No	BILLS	DUE DATES	BUDGET	REALIZATION

NOTES

{MONTHLY BUDGET}

STARTING BALANCE   STARTING DEBT   MONTHLY INCOME

_____   _____   _____

{EXPENSES}

HOUSING	BUDGET	SPENT	TRANSPORTATION	BUDGET	SPENT
Rent/Mortgage			Car Payment		
Taxes			Car Insurance		
Insurance			Gas		
Repairs			Maintenance		
Total			Total		

UTILITIES	BUDGET	SPENT	PERSONAL	BUDGET	SPENT
Electricity			Entertainment		
Gas			Clothing		
Sewer/Trash			Kids Stuff		
Internet			Cosmetic		
Phone			Medical		
Total			Total		

FOOD	BUDGET	SPENT	MEDICAL	BUDGET	SPENT
Grocery			Doctor Bills		
Restaurants			Medication		
Total			Total		

CHARITY	BUDGET	SPENT	DEBTS	BUDGET	SPENT
Tithes			CC 1		
Charity			CC 2		
Total			Total		

STARTING BALANCE   STARTING DEBT   MONTHLY INCOME

_____   _____   _____

{FILE IT}

MONEY

TAXES

MEDICAL

HOME

AUTO

BUSINESS

Bills Payment Schedule & List

PAID Yes/No	BILLS	DUE DATES	BUDGET	REALIZATION

NOTES

Bills Payment Schedule & List

PAID Yes/No	BILLS	DUE DATES	BUDGET	REALIZATION

NOTES

_____
_____
_____
_____
_____
_____

{MONTHLY BUDGET}

STARTING BALANCE	STARTING DEBT	MONTHLY INCOME
_____	_____	_____

{EXPENSES}

HOUSING	BUDGET	SPENT	TRANSPORTATION	BUDGET	SPENT
Rent/Mortgage			Car Payment		
Taxes			Car Insurance		
Insurance			Gas		
Repairs			Maintenance		
Total			Total		

UTILITIES	BUDGET	SPENT	PERSONAL	BUDGET	SPENT
Electricity			Entertainment		
Gas			Clothing		
Sewer/Trash			Kids Stuff		
Internet			Cosmetic		
Phone			Medical		
Total			Total		

FOOD	BUDGET	SPENT	MEDICAL	BUDGET	SPENT
Grocery			Doctor Bills		
Restaurants			Medication		
Total			Total		

CHARITY	BUDGET	SPENT	DEBTS	BUDGET	SPENT
Tithes			CC 1		
Charity			CC 2		
Total			Total		

STARTING BALANCE	STARTING DEBT	MONTHLY INCOME
_____	_____	_____

{FILE IT}

MONEY

TAXES

MEDICAL

HOME

AUTO

BUSINESS

Bills Payment Schedule & List

PAID Yes/No	BILLS	DUE DATES	BUDGET	REALIZATION

NOTES

_____
_____
_____
_____
_____
_____

Bills Payment Schedule & List

PAID Yes/No	BILLS	DUE DATES	BUDGET	REALIZATION

NOTES
_____
_____
_____
_____
_____
_____

{MONTHLY BUDGET}

STARTING BALANCE	STARTING DEBT	MONTHLY INCOME

{EXPENSES}

HOUSING	BUDGET	SPENT	TRANSPORTATION	BUDGET	SPENT
Rent/Mortgage			Car Payment		
Taxes			Car Insurance		
Insurance			Gas		
Repairs			Maintenance		
Total			Total		

UTILITIES	BUDGET	SPENT	PERSONAL	BUDGET	SPENT
Electricity			Entertainment		
Gas			Clothing		
Sewer/Trash			Kids Stuff		
Internet			Cosmetic		
Phone			Medical		
Total			Total		

FOOD	BUDGET	SPENT	MEDICAL	BUDGET	SPENT
Grocery			Doctor Bills		
Restaurants			Medication		
Total			Total		

CHARITY	BUDGET	SPENT	DEBTS	BUDGET	SPENT
Tithes			CC 1		
Charity			CC 2		
Total			Total		

STARTING BALANCE	STARTING DEBT	MONTHLY INCOME

{FILE IT}

MONEY

TAXES

MEDICAL

HOME

AUTO

BUSINESS

Bills Payment Schedule & List

PAID Yes/No	BILLS	DUE DATES	BUDGET	REALIZATION

NOTES

_____

_____

_____

_____

_____

_____

Bills Payment Schedule & List

PAID Yes/No	BILLS	DUE DATES	BUDGET	REALIZATION

NOTES

{MONTHLY BUDGET}

STARTING BALANCE	STARTING DEBT	MONTHLY INCOME
_____	_____	_____

{EXPENSES}

HOUSING	BUDGET	SPENT	TRANSPORTATION	BUDGET	SPENT
Rent/Mortgage			Car Payment		
Taxes			Car Insurance		
Insurance			Gas		
Repairs			Maintenance		
Total			Total		

UTILITIES	BUDGET	SPENT	PERSONAL	BUDGET	SPENT
Electricity			Entertainment		
Gas			Clothing		
Sewer/Trash			Kids Stuff		
Internet			Cosmetic		
Phone			Medical		
Total			Total		

FOOD	BUDGET	SPENT	MEDICAL	BUDGET	SPENT
Grocery			Doctor Bills		
Restaurants			Medication		
Total			Total		

CHARITY	BUDGET	SPENT	DEBTS	BUDGET	SPENT
Tithes			CC 1		
Charity			CC 2		
Total			Total		

STARTING BALANCE	STARTING DEBT	MONTHLY INCOME
_____	_____	_____

{FILE IT}

MONEY

TAXES

MEDICAL

HOME

AUTO

BUSINESS

Bills Payment Schedule & List

PAID Yes/No	BILLS	DUE DATES	BUDGET	REALIZATION

NOTES

_____

_____

_____

_____

_____

_____

Bills Payment Schedule & List

PAID Yes/No	BILLS	DUE DATES	BUDGET	REALIZATION

NOTES

_____
_____
_____
_____
_____
_____

{MONTHLY BUDGET}

STARTING BALANCE	STARTING DEBT	MONTHLY INCOME
_____	_____	_____

{EXPENSES}

HOUSING	BUDGET	SPENT	TRANSPORTATION	BUDGET	SPENT
Rent/Mortgage			Car Payment		
Taxes			Car Insurance		
Insurance			Gas		
Repairs			Maintenance		
Total			Total		

UTILITIES	BUDGET	SPENT	PERSONAL	BUDGET	SPENT
Electricity			Entertainment		
Gas			Clothing		
Sewer/Trash			Kids Stuff		
Internet			Cosmetic		
Phone			Medical		
Total			Total		

FOOD	BUDGET	SPENT	MEDICAL	BUDGET	SPENT
Grocery			Doctor Bills		
Restaurants			Medication		
Total			Total		

CHARITY	BUDGET	SPENT	DEBTS	BUDGET	SPENT
Tithes			CC 1		
Charity			CC 2		
Total			Total		

STARTING BALANCE	STARTING DEBT	MONTHLY INCOME
_____	_____	_____

{FILE IT}

MONEY

TAXES

MEDICAL

HOME

AUTO

BUSINESS

Bills Payment Schedule & List

PAID Yes/No	BILLS	DUE DATES	BUDGET	REALIZATION

NOTES

_____

_____

_____

_____

_____

_____

Bills Payment Schedule & List

PAID Yes/No	BILLS	DUE DATES	BUDGET	REALIZATION

NOTES

{MONTHLY BUDGET}

STARTING BALANCE	STARTING DEBT	MONTHLY INCOME
_____	_____	_____

{EXPENSES}

HOUSING	BUDGET	SPENT	TRANSPORTATION	BUDGET	SPENT
Rent/Mortgage			Car Payment		
Taxes			Car Insurance		
Insurance			Gas		
Repairs			Maintenance		
Total			Total		

UTILITIES	BUDGET	SPENT	PERSONAL	BUDGET	SPENT
Electricity			Entertainment		
Gas			Clothing		
Sewer/Trash			Kids Stuff		
Internet			Cosmetic		
Phone			Medical		
Total			Total		

FOOD	BUDGET	SPENT	MEDICAL	BUDGET	SPENT
Grocery			Doctor Bills		
Restaurants			Medication		
Total			Total		

CHARITY	BUDGET	SPENT	DEBTS	BUDGET	SPENT
Tithes			CC 1		
Charity			CC 2		
Total			Total		

STARTING BALANCE	STARTING DEBT	MONTHLY INCOME
_____	_____	_____

{FILE IT}

MONEY

TAXES

MEDICAL

HOME

AUTO

BUSINESS

Bills Payment Schedule & List

PAID Yes/No	BILLS	DUE DATES	BUDGET	REALIZATION

NOTES
_____
_____
_____
_____
_____
_____

Bills Payment Schedule & List

PAID Yes/No	BILLS	DUE DATES	BUDGET	REALIZATION

NOTES

_____
_____
_____
_____
_____
_____

{MONTHLY BUDGET}

STARTING BALANCE	STARTING DEBT	MONTHLY INCOME
_____	_____	_____

{EXPENSES}

HOUSING	BUDGET	SPENT	TRANSPORTATION	BUDGET	SPENT
Rent/Mortgage			Car Payment		
Taxes			Car Insurance		
Insurance			Gas		
Repairs			Maintenance		
Total			Total		

UTILITIES	BUDGET	SPENT	PERSONAL	BUDGET	SPENT
Electricity			Entertainment		
Gas			Clothing		
Sewer/Trash			Kids Stuff		
Internet			Cosmetic		
Phone			Medical		
Total			Total		

FOOD	BUDGET	SPENT	MEDICAL	BUDGET	SPENT
Grocery			Doctor Bills		
Restaurants			Medication		
Total			Total		

CHARITY	BUDGET	SPENT	DEBTS	BUDGET	SPENT
Tithes			CC 1		
Charity			CC 2		
Total			Total		

STARTING BALANCE	STARTING DEBT	MONTHLY INCOME
_____	_____	_____

{FILE IT}

MONEY

TAXES

MEDICAL

HOME

AUTO

BUSINESS

Bills Payment Schedule & List

PAID Yes/No	BILLS	DUE DATES	BUDGET	REALIZATION

NOTES
_____
_____
_____
_____
_____
_____

Bills Payment Schedule & List

PAID Yes/No	BILLS	DUE DATES	BUDGET	REALIZATION

NOTES

_____
_____
_____
_____
_____
_____

{MONTHLY BUDGET}

STARTING BALANCE	STARTING DEBT	MONTHLY INCOME
_____	_____	_____

{EXPENSES}

HOUSING	BUDGET	SPENT	TRANSPORTATION	BUDGET	SPENT
Rent/Mortgage			Car Payment		
Taxes			Car Insurance		
Insurance			Gas		
Repairs			Maintenance		
Total			Total		

UTILITIES	BUDGET	SPENT	PERSONAL	BUDGET	SPENT
Electricity			Entertainment		
Gas			Clothing		
Sewer/Trash			Kids Stuff		
Internet			Cosmetic		
Phone			Medical		
Total			Total		

FOOD	BUDGET	SPENT	MEDICAL	BUDGET	SPENT
Grocery			Doctor Bills		
Restaurants			Medication		
Total			Total		

CHARITY	BUDGET	SPENT	DEBTS	BUDGET	SPENT
Tithes			CC 1		
Charity			CC 2		
Total			Total		

STARTING BALANCE	STARTING DEBT	MONTHLY INCOME
_____	_____	_____

{FILE IT}

MONEY

TAXES

MEDICAL

HOME

AUTO

BUSINESS

Bills Payment Schedule & List

PAID Yes/No	BILLS	DUE DATES	BUDGET	REALIZATION

NOTES

_____

_____

_____

_____

_____

_____

Bills Payment Schedule & List

PAID Yes/No	BILLS	DUE DATES	BUDGET	REALIZATION

NOTES

{MONTHLY BUDGET}

STARTING BALANCE	STARTING DEBT	MONTHLY INCOME

{EXPENSES}

HOUSING	BUDGET	SPENT	TRANSPORTATION	BUDGET	SPENT
Rent/Mortgage			Car Payment		
Taxes			Car Insurance		
Insurance			Gas		
Repairs			Maintenance		
Total			Total		

UTILITIES	BUDGET	SPENT	PERSONAL	BUDGET	SPENT
Electricity			Entertainment		
Gas			Clothing		
Sewer/Trash			Kids Stuff		
Internet			Cosmetic		
Phone			Medical		
Total			Total		

FOOD	BUDGET	SPENT	MEDICAL	BUDGET	SPENT
Grocery			Doctor Bills		
Restaurants			Medication		
Total			Total		

CHARITY	BUDGET	SPENT	DEBTS	BUDGET	SPENT
Tithes			CC 1		
Charity			CC 2		
Total			Total		

STARTING BALANCE	STARTING DEBT	MONTHLY INCOME

{FILE IT}

MONEY

TAXES

MEDICAL

HOME

AUTO

BUSINESS

Bills Payment Schedule & List

PAID Yes/No	BILLS	DUE DATES	BUDGET	REALIZATION

NOTES

Bills Payment Schedule & List

PAID Yes/No	BILLS	DUE DATES	BUDGET	REALIZATION

NOTES

_____

_____

_____

_____

_____

_____

{MONTHLY BUDGET}

STARTING BALANCE	STARTING DEBT	MONTHLY INCOME
_____	_____	_____

{EXPENSES}

HOUSING	BUDGET	SPENT	TRANSPORTATION	BUDGET	SPENT
Rent/Mortgage			Car Payment		
Taxes			Car Insurance		
Insurance			Gas		
Repairs			Maintenance		
Total			Total		

UTILITIES	BUDGET	SPENT	PERSONAL	BUDGET	SPENT
Electricity			Entertainment		
Gas			Clothing		
Sewer/Trash			Kids Stuff		
Internet			Cosmetic		
Phone			Medical		
Total			Total		

FOOD	BUDGET	SPENT	MEDICAL	BUDGET	SPENT
Grocery			Doctor Bills		
Restaurants			Medication		
Total			Total		

CHARITY	BUDGET	SPENT	DEBTS	BUDGET	SPENT
Tithes			CC 1		
Charity			CC 2		
Total			Total		

STARTING BALANCE	STARTING DEBT	MONTHLY INCOME
_____	_____	_____

{FILE IT}

MONEY

TAXES

MEDICAL

HOME

AUTO

BUSINESS

Bills Payment Schedule & List

PAID Yes/No	BILLS	DUE DATES	BUDGET	REALIZATION

NOTES

_____

_____

_____

_____

_____

_____

Bills Payment Schedule & List

PAID Yes/No	BILLS	DUE DATES	BUDGET	REALIZATION

NOTES

_____
_____
_____
_____
_____
_____

{MONTHLY BUDGET}

STARTING BALANCE	STARTING DEBT	MONTHLY INCOME
_____	_____	_____

{EXPENSES}

HOUSING	BUDGET	SPENT	TRANSPORTATION	BUDGET	SPENT
Rent/Mortgage			Car Payment		
Taxes			Car Insurance		
Insurance			Gas		
Repairs			Maintenance		
Total			Total		

UTILITIES	BUDGET	SPENT	PERSONAL	BUDGET	SPENT
Electricity			Entertainment		
Gas			Clothing		
Sewer/Trash			Kids Stuff		
Internet			Cosmetic		
Phone			Medical		
Total			Total		

FOOD	BUDGET	SPENT	MEDICAL	BUDGET	SPENT
Grocery			Doctor Bills		
Restaurants			Medication		
Total			Total		

CHARITY	BUDGET	SPENT	DEBTS	BUDGET	SPENT
Tithes			CC 1		
Charity			CC 2		
Total			Total		

STARTING BALANCE	STARTING DEBT	MONTHLY INCOME
_____	_____	_____

{FILE IT}

MONEY

TAXES

MEDICAL

HOME

AUTO

BUSINESS

Bills Payment Schedule & List

PAID Yes/No	BILLS	DUE DATES	BUDGET	REALIZATION

NOTES

_____

_____

_____

_____

_____

_____

Bills Payment Schedule & List

PAID Yes/No	BILLS	DUE DATES	BUDGET	REALIZATION

NOTES

{MONTHLY BUDGET}

STARTING BALANCE	STARTING DEBT	MONTHLY INCOME
_____	_____	_____

{EXPENSES}

HOUSING	BUDGET	SPENT	TRANSPORTATION	BUDGET	SPENT
Rent/Mortgage			Car Payment		
Taxes			Car Insurance		
Insurance			Gas		
Repairs			Maintenance		
Total			Total		

UTILITIES	BUDGET	SPENT	PERSONAL	BUDGET	SPENT
Electricity			Entertainment		
Gas			Clothing		
Sewer/Trash			Kids Stuff		
Internet			Cosmetic		
Phone			Medical		
Total			Total		

FOOD	BUDGET	SPENT	MEDICAL	BUDGET	SPENT
Grocery			Doctor Bills		
Restaurants			Medication		
Total			Total		

CHARITY	BUDGET	SPENT	DEBTS	BUDGET	SPENT
Tithes			CC 1		
Charity			CC 2		
Total			Total		

STARTING BALANCE	STARTING DEBT	MONTHLY INCOME
_____	_____	_____

{FILE IT}

MONEY

TAXES

MEDICAL

HOME

AUTO

BUSINESS

Bills Payment Schedule & List

PAID Yes/No	BILLS	DUE DATES	BUDGET	REALIZATION

NOTES

Bills Payment Schedule & List

PAID Yes/No	BILLS	DUE DATES	BUDGET	REALIZATION

NOTES

_____

_____

_____

_____

_____

_____

{MONTHLY BUDGET}

STARTING BALANCE	STARTING DEBT	MONTHLY INCOME
_____	_____	_____

{EXPENSES}

HOUSING	BUDGET	SPENT	TRANSPORTATION	BUDGET	SPENT
Rent/Mortgage			Car Payment		
Taxes			Car Insurance		
Insurance			Gas		
Repairs			Maintenance		
Total			Total		

UTILITIES	BUDGET	SPENT	PERSONAL	BUDGET	SPENT
Electricity			Entertainment		
Gas			Clothing		
Sewer/Trash			Kids Stuff		
Internet			Cosmetic		
Phone			Medical		
Total			Total		

FOOD	BUDGET	SPENT	MEDICAL	BUDGET	SPENT
Grocery			Doctor Bills		
Restaurants			Medication		
Total			Total		

CHARITY	BUDGET	SPENT	DEBTS	BUDGET	SPENT
Tithes			CC 1		
Charity			CC 2		
Total			Total		

STARTING BALANCE	STARTING DEBT	MONTHLY INCOME
_____	_____	_____

{FILE IT}

MONEY

TAXES

MEDICAL

HOME

AUTO

BUSINESS

Bills Payment Schedule & List

PAID Yes/No	BILLS	DUE DATES	BUDGET	REALIZATION

NOTES

_____
_____
_____
_____
_____
_____

Bills Payment Schedule & List

PAID Yes/No	BILLS	DUE DATES	BUDGET	REALIZATION

NOTES

_____

_____

_____

_____

_____

_____

{MONTHLY BUDGET}

STARTING BALANCE	STARTING DEBT	MONTHLY INCOME

{EXPENSES}

HOUSING	BUDGET	SPENT	TRANSPORTATION	BUDGET	SPENT
Rent/Mortgage			Car Payment		
Taxes			Car Insurance		
Insurance			Gas		
Repairs			Maintenance		
Total			Total		

UTILITIES	BUDGET	SPENT	PERSONAL	BUDGET	SPENT
Electricity			Entertainment		
Gas			Clothing		
Sewer/Trash			Kids Stuff		
Internet			Cosmetic		
Phone			Medical		
Total			Total		

FOOD	BUDGET	SPENT	MEDICAL	BUDGET	SPENT
Grocery			Doctor Bills		
Restaurants			Medication		
Total			Total		

CHARITY	BUDGET	SPENT	DEBTS	BUDGET	SPENT
Tithes			CC 1		
Charity			CC 2		
Total			Total		

STARTING BALANCE	STARTING DEBT	MONTHLY INCOME

{FILE IT}

MONEY

TAXES

MEDICAL

HOME

AUTO

BUSINESS

Bills Payment Schedule & List

PAID Yes/No	BILLS	DUE DATES	BUDGET	REALIZATION

NOTES
_____
_____
_____
_____
_____
_____

Bills Payment Schedule & List

PAID Yes/No	BILLS	DUE DATES	BUDGET	REALIZATION

NOTES

_____
_____
_____
_____
_____
_____

{MONTHLY BUDGET}

STARTING BALANCE	STARTING DEBT	MONTHLY INCOME
_____	_____	_____

{EXPENSES}

HOUSING	BUDGET	SPENT	TRANSPORTATION	BUDGET	SPENT
Rent/Mortgage			Car Payment		
Taxes			Car Insurance		
Insurance			Gas		
Repairs			Maintenance		
Total			Total		

UTILITIES	BUDGET	SPENT	PERSONAL	BUDGET	SPENT
Electricity			Entertainment		
Gas			Clothing		
Sewer/Trash			Kids Stuff		
Internet			Cosmetic		
Phone			Medical		
Total			Total		

FOOD	BUDGET	SPENT	MEDICAL	BUDGET	SPENT
Grocery			Doctor Bills		
Restaurants			Medication		
Total			Total		

CHARITY	BUDGET	SPENT	DEBTS	BUDGET	SPENT
Tithes			CC 1		
Charity			CC 2		
Total			Total		

STARTING BALANCE	STARTING DEBT	MONTHLY INCOME
_____	_____	_____

{FILE IT}

MONEY

TAXES

MEDICAL

HOME

AUTO

BUSINESS

Bills Payment Schedule & List

PAID Yes/No	BILLS	DUE DATES	BUDGET	REALIZATION

NOTES

Bills Payment Schedule & List

PAID Yes/No	BILLS	DUE DATES	BUDGET	REALIZATION

NOTES

{MONTHLY BUDGET}

STARTING BALANCE	STARTING DEBT	MONTHLY INCOME
_____	_____	_____

{EXPENSES}

HOUSING	BUDGET	SPENT	TRANSPORTATION	BUDGET	SPENT
Rent/Mortgage			Car Payment		
Taxes			Car Insurance		
Insurance			Gas		
Repairs			Maintenance		
Total			Total		

UTILITIES	BUDGET	SPENT	PERSONAL	BUDGET	SPENT
Electricity			Entertainment		
Gas			Clothing		
Sewer/Trash			Kids Stuff		
Internet			Cosmetic		
Phone			Medical		
Total			Total		

FOOD	BUDGET	SPENT	MEDICAL	BUDGET	SPENT
Grocery			Doctor Bills		
Restaurants			Medication		
Total			Total		

CHARITY	BUDGET	SPENT	DEBTS	BUDGET	SPENT
Tithes			CC 1		
Charity			CC 2		
Total			Total		

STARTING BALANCE	STARTING DEBT	MONTHLY INCOME
_____	_____	_____

{FILE IT}

MONEY

TAXES

MEDICAL

HOME

AUTO

BUSINESS

Bills Payment Schedule & List

PAID Yes/No	BILLS	DUE DATES	BUDGET	REALIZATION

NOTES

_____

_____

_____

_____

_____

_____

Bills Payment Schedule & List

PAID Yes/No	BILLS	DUE DATES	BUDGET	REALIZATION

NOTES

_____
_____
_____
_____
_____
_____

{MONTHLY BUDGET}

STARTING BALANCE	STARTING DEBT	MONTHLY INCOME
_____	_____	_____

{EXPENSES}

HOUSING	BUDGET	SPENT	TRANSPORTATION	BUDGET	SPENT
Rent/Mortgage			Car Payment		
Taxes			Car Insurance		
Insurance			Gas		
Repairs			Maintenance		
Total			Total		

UTILITIES	BUDGET	SPENT	PERSONAL	BUDGET	SPENT
Electricity			Entertainment		
Gas			Clothing		
Sewer/Trash			Kids Stuff		
Internet			Cosmetic		
Phone			Medical		
Total			Total		

FOOD	BUDGET	SPENT	MEDICAL	BUDGET	SPENT
Grocery			Doctor Bills		
Restaurants			Medication		
Total			Total		

CHARITY	BUDGET	SPENT	DEBTS	BUDGET	SPENT
Tithes			CC 1		
Charity			CC 2		
Total			Total		

STARTING BALANCE	STARTING DEBT	MONTHLY INCOME
_____	_____	_____

{FILE IT}

MONEY

TAXES

MEDICAL

HOME

AUTO

BUSINESS

Bills Payment Schedule & List

PAID Yes/No	BILLS	DUE DATES	BUDGET	REALIZATION

NOTES

_____

_____

_____

_____

_____

_____

Bills Payment Schedule & List

PAID Yes/No	BILLS	DUE DATES	BUDGET	REALIZATION

NOTES

_____

_____

_____

_____

_____

_____

{MONTHLY BUDGET}

STARTING BALANCE	STARTING DEBT	MONTHLY INCOME

{EXPENSES}

HOUSING	BUDGET	SPENT	TRANSPORTATION	BUDGET	SPENT
Rent/Mortgage			Car Payment		
Taxes			Car Insurance		
Insurance			Gas		
Repairs			Maintenance		
Total			Total		

UTILITIES	BUDGET	SPENT	PERSONAL	BUDGET	SPENT
Electricity			Entertainment		
Gas			Clothing		
Sewer/Trash			Kids Stuff		
Internet			Cosmetic		
Phone			Medical		
Total			Total		

FOOD	BUDGET	SPENT	MEDICAL	BUDGET	SPENT
Grocery			Doctor Bills		
Restaurants			Medication		
Total			Total		

CHARITY	BUDGET	SPENT	DEBTS	BUDGET	SPENT
Tithes			CC 1		
Charity			CC 2		
Total			Total		

STARTING BALANCE	STARTING DEBT	MONTHLY INCOME

{FILE IT}

MONEY

TAXES

MEDICAL

HOME

AUTO

BUSINESS

Bills Payment Schedule & List

PAID Yes/No	BILLS	DUE DATES	BUDGET	REALIZATION

NOTES

_____
_____
_____
_____
_____
_____

Bills Payment Schedule & List

PAID Yes/No	BILLS	DUE DATES	BUDGET	REALIZATION

NOTES
_____
_____
_____
_____
_____
_____

{MONTHLY BUDGET}

STARTING BALANCE	STARTING DEBT	MONTHLY INCOME

{EXPENSES}

HOUSING	BUDGET	SPENT	TRANSPORTATION	BUDGET	SPENT
Rent/Mortgage			Car Payment		
Taxes			Car Insurance		
Insurance			Gas		
Repairs			Maintenance		
Total			Total		

UTILITIES	BUDGET	SPENT	PERSONAL	BUDGET	SPENT
Electricity			Entertainment		
Gas			Clothing		
Sewer/Trash			Kids Stuff		
Internet			Cosmetic		
Phone			Medical		
Total			Total		

FOOD	BUDGET	SPENT	MEDICAL	BUDGET	SPENT
Grocery			Doctor Bills		
Restaurants			Medication		
Total			Total		

CHARITY	BUDGET	SPENT	DEBTS	BUDGET	SPENT
Tithes			CC 1		
Charity			CC 2		
Total			Total		

STARTING BALANCE	STARTING DEBT	MONTHLY INCOME

{FILE IT}

MONEY

TAXES

MEDICAL

HOME

AUTO

BUSINESS

Bills Payment Schedule & List

PAID Yes/No	BILLS	DUE DATES	BUDGET	REALIZATION

NOTES

_____

_____

_____

_____

_____

_____

Bills Payment Schedule & List

PAID Yes/No	BILLS	DUE DATES	BUDGET	REALIZATION

NOTES

_____
_____
_____
_____
_____
_____

{MONTHLY BUDGET}

STARTING BALANCE	STARTING DEBT	MONTHLY INCOME

{EXPENSES}

HOUSING	BUDGET	SPENT	TRANSPORTATION	BUDGET	SPENT
Rent/Mortgage			Car Payment		
Taxes			Car Insurance		
Insurance			Gas		
Repairs			Maintenance		
Total			Total		

UTILITIES	BUDGET	SPENT	PERSONAL	BUDGET	SPENT
Electricity			Entertainment		
Gas			Clothing		
Sewer/Trash			Kids Stuff		
Internet			Cosmetic		
Phone			Medical		
Total			Total		

FOOD	BUDGET	SPENT	MEDICAL	BUDGET	SPENT
Grocery			Doctor Bills		
Restaurants			Medication		
Total			Total		

CHARITY	BUDGET	SPENT	DEBTS	BUDGET	SPENT
Tithes			CC 1		
Charity			CC 2		
Total			Total		

STARTING BALANCE	STARTING DEBT	MONTHLY INCOME

{FILE IT}

MONEY

TAXES

MEDICAL

HOME

AUTO

BUSINESS

Bills Payment Schedule & List

PAID Yes/No	BILLS	DUE DATES	BUDGET	REALIZATION

NOTES

_____

_____

_____

_____

_____

_____

Bills Payment Schedule & List

PAID Yes/No	BILLS	DUE DATES	BUDGET	REALIZATION

NOTES

_____
_____
_____
_____
_____
_____

{MONTHLY BUDGET}

STARTING BALANCE	STARTING DEBT	MONTHLY INCOME
_____	_____	_____

{EXPENSES}

HOUSING	BUDGET	SPENT	TRANSPORTATION	BUDGET	SPENT
Rent/Mortgage			Car Payment		
Taxes			Car Insurance		
Insurance			Gas		
Repairs			Maintenance		
Total			Total		

UTILITIES	BUDGET	SPENT	PERSONAL	BUDGET	SPENT
Electricity			Entertainment		
Gas			Clothing		
Sewer/Trash			Kids Stuff		
Internet			Cosmetic		
Phone			Medical		
Total			Total		

FOOD	BUDGET	SPENT	MEDICAL	BUDGET	SPENT
Grocery			Doctor Bills		
Restaurants			Medication		
Total			Total		

CHARITY	BUDGET	SPENT	DEBTS	BUDGET	SPENT
Tithes			CC 1		
Charity			CC 2		
Total			Total		

STARTING BALANCE	STARTING DEBT	MONTHLY INCOME
_____	_____	_____

{FILE IT}

MONEY

TAXES

MEDICAL

HOME

AUTO

BUSINESS

Bills Payment Schedule & List

PAID Yes/No	BILLS	DUE DATES	BUDGET	REALIZATION

NOTES

_____

_____

_____

_____

_____

_____

Bills Payment Schedule & List

PAID Yes/No	BILLS	DUE DATES	BUDGET	REALIZATION

NOTES

www.ingramcontent.com/pod-product-compliance
Lightning Source LLC
Chambersburg PA
CBHW081335090426
42737CB00017B/3154